The Nocturnal Genius

All rights Reserved. Copyright Of
Alexander Montrose ©

Contents

CHAPTER 1: INSOMNIA IS A BLESSING IN DISGUISE 1
    INSOMNIA AND IQ 3
CHAPTER 2: SYMPTOMS OF SUCCESS 7
    THE URGE TO SEIZE THE MOMENT BUT EVERYTHING IS ALWAYS CLOSED? 7
CHAPTER 3: AWAKE WHILST OTHERS ARE ASLEEP 11
CHAPTER 4: SEEING 2 AM MORE THAN 2 PM 15
    OWLS AND LARKS 16
CHAPTER 5: INSPIRED BY THE QUIETER HOURS OF THE DAY 21
    HARMFUL NOISE AND WORKERS 26
    FIVE QUIET TIME BENEFITS 28
CHAPTER 6: ARE THE HOURS DRAGGING PAST WITHOUT PURPOSE? 32
    RACING THOUGHTS AND INSOMNIA CAUSES 32
    HOW TO EASE THE THINKING OF RACING 34
    HOW TO USE 'PLANED TIME OF WORK' 34
    DOWNHILL BEFORE BEDTIME 35
CHAPTER 7: DON'T JUST SURVIVE THE NIGHT, LEARN TO THRIVE
AND *BECOME A HUNTER.* 37
    EXERCISE 40
CHAPTER 8: BEING A NIGHT OWL IS RESILIENT, EMPOWERING
AND REWARDING 41
    RECOGNIZE THAT NATURE IS NOT FOOD 41
    ENABLING YOURSELF 42
    BEAR IN MIND 42
    RECOGNIZE YOURSELF 43
    MAKE ACCEPTANCE 43
    FIND THE RIGHT ECONOMY 44

CHAPTER 9: BREAKTHROUGH IDEAS 45

CHAPTER 10: DELIBERATE INNOVATING. 47

CHAPTER 11: HOW ABOUT THAT SIDE HUSTLE THAT EVERY MORNING PERSON PUT YOU DOWN ON? 49

    GET ORGANIZED 50
    VALUE YOUR TIME LIKE AN INVESTMENT 50
    OWN IT 51
    KNOW THE TIME TO REST 51
    DO YOU WORK? 52

CHAPTER 12: YOU ARE A NIGHT OWL, AND SOON TO BE A CREATURE OF SUCCESSFUL HABIT 53

    AT MORNINGS, WE ARE NOT JUST BAD: WE ARE DONE THAT WAY 55
    WHEN THE WORLD GOES TO SLEEP, IT IS EASIER TO BE PRODUCTIVE ... 56

CHAPTER 13: LIFE-CHANGING HABITS, VISIONS AND UNBREAKABLE LIFE GOALS. 60

    NIGHT OWL COPING AND HEALTH 61

CHAPTER 14: UNLIMITED, EFFORTLESS METHODS 63

CHAPTER 1:

Insomnia is a Blessing in Disguise

Did you know that Leonardo da Vinci slept in cycles of twenty-minute naps, every four hours during a single day? That's just two total sleep hours! Maybe it's not in stone, but psychology today tells us intelligent people are more likely to be night owls. The question is: Do owls have higher IQs at night? Does a night thinker thrive above a morning riser? Check out the five fascinating facts that will convince you that being a night owl may be of an advantage in our modern society.

Last midnight — Human IQ Golden Hour(s).

Psychology Today, clever people are likely to be nightlife with a higher IQ bed later on both weekdays and weekends. Psychologist Satoshi Kanazawa and Study Magazine further pointed out that individuals with an average IQ usually sleep about 12:10 am in their 20s. In contrast, those with a lower IQ were gone to bed around 11:41 pm. The ones designated "extremely luminous" hit the sack at 12:29 a.m.

Intelligent or deviant?

The psychologist Kanazawa Study Magazine also claims that persons who have a higher intelligence may follow a pattern of not following the crowds, which began in ancient times. After all, in the night by the fire, there wasn't much to do except think. If this is a protest against the current schedules of 9 to 5, the high IQ individual would extend – not shorten – his day. They usually work early and work longer.

Afterdark, daydreaming.

Daydreaming can be challenging throughout the day, with many distractions with work, children, friends and daytime hours duties. Some research shows that higher IQ hours such as 11 pm onwards induce a calm, conducive, wandering mind. (The treasure trove of great ideas)

Patterns of inherited sleep... and hereditary IQ.

Scientists think that 50% of our sleep pattern is hereditary. Given that IQ and intelligence may potentially be inherited, is it possible that IQ with a night sleep pattern is transmitted? What makes a night owl - intelligence, genes, or simple habits are challenging to identify. But owls at night would indeed tell you it's challenging to become morning larks.

The drawbacks of an owl at night.

Sleep is a necessary health aspect. In the Kanazawa study, persons tended to be susceptible to disease, heart failure and sadness. According to another psychologist, Marian Giamnietro, addictions and eating disorders are less steady, less trustworthy and more likely.

Insomnia and IQ

THE SCIENCE

A multitude of scientific studies reveals that IQ has a percentage correlation with insomnia.

Society tells us, trains us, to be morning people, catch that early morning worm and thrive. This statement is fundamentally flawed. Thousands, if not millions of human beings remain in this primitive cycle for the dominant part of their life, and very few can break through this glass ceiling. When they rise in the morning, they answer to society and their bosses but when you are a night owl, you work for nobody and answer to no one.

Early results

A study employing Cambridge Brain Science (CBS) Trials examined the biological foundation of intelligence. Previously, sleep spindles, which are brief brain periodic fluctuations during the sleep process, were connected to the IQ test results. In the latest study, published in the Cognitive Neuroscience Journal, Fang, Sergeeva, Ray, Viczko, Owen and Fogel, tried to answer these questions. They had participants sleeping in the lab while physiological data was being gathered, including sleep quality assessments and sleep spindle features. The results imply that these specific bumps of brain activity during sleep are closely interconnected with "*fluid intelligence*" evaluated by the ability to reason.

Dr Rachel Salas, an Assistant Neurology Professor of the Johns Hopkins University School of Medicine, and colleagues studied how, using an approach called transcranial magnetic stimulation, brains of 18 insomniacs and 10 good sleepers were plastic or flexible. In comparison to good sleepers, *the insomniacs showed increased brain activity.* Indeed, people with insomnia have shown more adaptability to take on heavier, complex workloads.

A significant amount of study has been underway in the last few decades into the relationship between sleep patterns and intelligence. A study was conducted by U.S. Air Force recruits, to examine the relationship between intelligence and sleep planning methodically. After assessing 420 participants, scientists found those night owls tend to have higher intelligence ratings. There is an identifiable presumption in many studies in the last decade which presumes that night owls are a direct result of insomnia.

Satoshi Kanazawa and Kaja Perinawas performed a study in 2009 entitled *"Why night owls are smarter."* He and his team concluded that:

"More clever youngsters are more likely to grow into night people, who go to bed late and rise late, both on weekdays and weekends."

The 2014 analysis of GMAT scores amongst MBA students by a team of scientists from Chicago University and Northwestern University. They found that the GMAT scores were much higher for owls at night than for men and women in the early morning.

The daily fall is about one IQ point in sleep loss for the first hour, two for the next, and four for the following. After five consecutive days without sleep, your IQ can be reduced by up to 15 points. This means that a person of normal intelligence can have an efficient IQ of only 85, which suggests that you require special training to learn.

Even a very 'intelligent' individual (120 plus IQ) can, as with an automated pilot, be reduced to robotic thinking.

The performance gap of an hour's sleep difference was greater than the gap between a normal fourth-grader and a typical sixth-grader. This is another way that a somewhat sleepy sixth-grader performs like a mere fourth grader in class. *"A one-hour sleep loss is tantamount to two years of cognitive maturation and development."*

A study employing CBS trials gave new insight into the biological foundation of intelligence. Sleep spindles – brief brain periodic fluctuation that occurs during non-fast eye movement sleep — have been previously linked to the performance of IQ tests. However, certain unsolved questions were raised:

- Sleep spindles are also linked to the quality of sleep because they defend against external stimulation. *Are they linked to IQ just because well-rested people tend to fare well in cognitive tests?*

- Intelligence, as we stated earlier, is not simply one thing. If sleep spindles are directly linked with overall intelligence, then which facet are they specifically linked to?

- These problems are addressed in the recent study by Fang, Sergeeva, Ray, Viczko, Owen and Fogel published in the Journal of Cognitive Neuroscience. They had people sleeping in a laboratory while physiological data were gathered, including sleep quality assessments and sleep spindle features. Later in the day, individuals performed a series of cognitive tests from CBS tests at their homes.

- The key consequence was that sleep spindles were indeed linked to cognitive performance and the relationship was not mediated by the quality of sleep. In addition, specifically, the connection between spindles and cognitive abilities was established. No correlations to verbal ability or short-term memory have been found. The results imply that these specific bumps of brain activity during sleep are closely interconnected with "fluid intelligence" evaluated by the ability to reason. But it's not only that people with specific spindles sleep better; it's not possible to explain the increase in thinking as a side effect of sleep quality.

- This is more a "wow, we have truly discovered something" than a "wow" insight, it will transform my life because sleeping spindles (like IQ) are quite stable and not under our control as far as we know. Sorry, counting spindles will probably not make you smarter instead than counting sheep.

- Due to each CBS trial's neural correlations, the researchers were also in a position to develop theories on the brain basis of the observed effects.

CHAPTER 2:

Symptoms of Success

The urge to seize the moment but everything is always closed?

At night, you may feel more productive. The hormone melatonin, which causes the body to feel less alert, diminishes later in the morning for owls at night. "Early in the day, they have their most productive. "Night types" tend late in the morning to wake up.

'Night owls' - people who are naturally late to wake up long past daybreak - had different brain activity patterns compared to 'morning larks' - found a new study. And these differences might make night owls' lives even harder if they have to keep to a regular 9-to-5 routine.

Night owls tend to be more creative and cognitive than their day friends. They are also more likely to explore the unknown, and by nature are more curious. Night owls are also risk-takers, which can lead to more successful and higher wages.

Are you the kind of person that stays up late in the night to read, write, tinker, or work? Are you best friends with your snooze button and loathe the so-called beauty of sunrise secretly? If you're a night owl, people could encourage you to go to bed earlier and learn "to be an adult." You could have an irritated supervisor, who doesn't understand why in the morning you're never on time. You may have a well-meaning buddy saying that you sleep more and quicken the phrase, "Early to bed, early rise, makes a man well, rich and wise." The thought that early waking up is a good thing is worthwhile. We can do chores during the early hours of the day to prevent exercise, meditation and studying entirely otherwise. But it is only because the early bird gets the worm that the owl of the night is left empty-handed. Studies suggest that night owls and people who wake up later are smarter and more creative than the early risers. They also possess higher Independent IQs. Unfortunately, night owls have less academic scores compared to early risers (by about 8%). This is likely because of all these differences between late-night creative types and early morning larks in brain chemistry. Your inclination to wake with the sun or to stay early in the morning is dictated by your DNA. Both groups require a full 8-hour quality sleep, but every group has a tremendous effect on its skills and experience on the other 16 hours. Here are five ways in which night owls come forward.

You have higher quantities

We have always had a defined circadian rhythm from an evolutionary point of view: waking up and falling asleep with the sun. Studies have indicated that people with higher IQs are likely to diverge from known developmental features, like circadian rhythms. Night owls who choose to wake up later in the day and stay awake, till the early hours of the morning, may be evolving. In any event, people with differing circadian cycles are deemed smarter than those with regular cycles of sleep.

They're less tired all day long

The greatest practical difference between early risers and night owls is the amount of time they maximize. Maximize early risers in the morning. They frequently wake up to work, get ready to work or work on hobbies before everyone else. On the other hand, night owls maximize the evenings. A recent study was conducted to find out when each group was strongest. They examined early risers and owls all day and found that night owls hit their peak vigour at 9 pm. Because each time is due to its central nervous system and spinal cord excitability. This provides owls with a rush of energy at night to send things like creative evenings, creativity and imagination into the world. On the other hand, early risers never reach this same level since their central nervous system and excitability of the spinal cord never fully line up at the same time. You reach a high at approximately 9:00 a.m. and then go downhill. When the early birds go asleep, the night owls are on their time. You will never start to slouch until you are ready to hit the pillow.

You're less stressed

People who wake up early will have higher cortisol levels, the principal stress hormone of the body, than people who fall asleep. People waking before 7:21 a.m. not only had higher levels of cortisol but also had higher levels all day long. Researchers have shown in a 10-week follow-up study with this same group that early risers are more likely to have muscle pain, headaches, and cold symptoms. They were also more likely than their owl counterparts to get furious throughout the day and weary by the end of the day.

You will experience creative breakthroughs more likely. The time of the evening is perfectly suitable for a creative breakthrough, whether if you feel like a night owl or not. When we're tired, our minds walk. This is the perfect chance to strike inspiration. We can follow distractions, and our tired mind is less likely to be caught up with the logistics of our ideas so that we might experience pure imagination. Early owls and early risers both benefit from this nocturnal creative power, but it is considerably less early to early risers.

There are no early risers for valuable hours

Earlier research has shown those night owls are smarter and richer compared to early risers, but current results reveal that they are faster and more alert when they complete complicated activities throughout the day. One study asked participants to keep their typical sleep cycles, with early risers falling to sleep roughly four hours before their night owls. These participants were then asked to carry out various activities, with researchers following their success. Both groups were clear and alert while they were up, but ten hours later early risers showed less attentive behaviour in areas of the brain. Although every group was up in the same length of time, night owls maximized their brain's capabilities all day, while the early risers had reduced cognitive performance. So the next time your best friend encourages you to go to bed "reasonably," you can be certain that your hour habits cost you nothing. In fact, they can be accountable for a higher IQ and a better and richer future. Ask Charles Darwin and Winston Churchill, the night owls were both well known and successful. The early bird could get the worm, but the night owls get a field full of unsuspecting mice. And who would like a worm anyway?

CHAPTER 3:

Awake whilst others are asleep

Are you shuddering with the simple concept of waking up early? You're a night owl—and that's probably how you were born. You call the scientific name of your preferred waking and sleep cycle your chronotype and it is partly regulated by your genes.

An early chronotype (also in the morning) has one main advantage: Their internal clock is closer to the timetables of school and works most days of the week. In fact, people with late chronotypes forced to adhere to a regular 9 to 5 schedule can experience the so-called social jet lag, despite their natural sleep preferences. And other studies indicate that early risers are linked to greater physical and mental health compared to late risers.

But owls of the night are not completely left behind. A mixture of scientific evidence shows certain specific advantages of having a late chronotype. Here are some of the most intriguing things to look at:

1. Maybe you're more creative.

Researchers in Italy classified 120 people as early birds, night owls, or something between them back in 2006. Each group then carried out a series of drawing tests to measure creative thinking. The later types also outpaced the early risers and people with moderate chronotypes.

One of the authors of the study believed that being an owl "may find the development of a non-conventional spirit and of the night of finding alternative and creative solutions," stated HuffPost.

2. You might be smarter.

In 2009, a study studied over 20,000 young people and showed that night owl was linked with a higher IQ. Even when researchers controlled other potential characteristics such as age, sex, income and education, this connection remained.

An earlier study by recruits from the US Air Force showed that evening owls had higher intelligence testing, and by 2014, another group of researchers revealed that night owls had higher testing rates in an MBA programme. (Take that, cheerful people in the morning!)

3. You may have better mental endurance than early birds.

The University of Liege in Belgium researchers have recruited 16 people in the morning and 15 in the night and let the two groups sleep on their own natural agenda. Then two mental alertness tests were conducted by both groups: one was taken 1.5 hours after waking, and the other 10.5 hours after waking.

According to the research published in the journal Science, both groups did equally well in the first test. But the second, later test showed that the night owls were roughly 6 percent better, which indicated that they were sharper after being awake for a long time.

4. You could obtain an extra burst of strength.

Night owls may want to hit the gym nearer to bedtime – at least according to a very tiny 2009 study. The researchers studied nine-night owls and nine early risers at different intervals of the day. In the morning, strength was constant regardless of time. The night, though, people had a burst of strength and peaked at night.

"We assumed people would be better in the morning this morning and never have changed it," Olle Lagerquist, co-author of the study, told CNN.

The scientists also noted that late in the day, people in the night experience "excitability" in the central nervous system, which may account for the added strength in the leg workouts, CNN said.

5. You could be better (truly!) at baseball.

This is a study of a small, super-selective population, but it's always fascinating. In 2011, researchers looked at 16 major League baseball players' hitting averages over a two full-season period. The players also completed a questionnaire determining whether they were a person in the morning or the evening.

The results showed that people were better off in games commencing at 14:00 in the morning than in the evening with a batting mean of 267. But when games start at 8 p.m., people had a significantly larger gap: they had a batting average of 306 at that time of the night, compared with people who hit 252. In other words: If every batter group has the opportunity to perform at its favourite time of day, the owls of the night blow the early birds out of the water. You could say that the night owls hit her out of the park (wink, wink).

CHAPTER 4:

Seeing 2 am more than 2 pm

Early birds were thought to get the worm, while evening owls had many advantages just because they were who they were. And now is the time for them to get some praise.

Please don't get us wrong: we are sleep advocates. And you must get the correct amount of sleep every day (7 to 9 hours for the normal adult), to keep you healthy. This is not allowing you to stay late and to sleep skimping. But if your lifestyle may make your wake time later, you may be encouraged to stay a little later too.

Although there's been considerable praise for being a morning person (these health benefits are true and very nice), there's not much to be done by being someone who works best in the evening. See — an ode for those who enjoy midnight oil burning.

While a start of 2:30 am would indicate a very long day, with no sleep, the early bedtime of Wahlberg shows that he runs for seven hours every night.

This is important for your productivity - your health and cognitive abilities have major consequences due to a lack of sleep.

This subject was discussed extensively by two American researchers, Christopher Barnes and Gretchen Spreitzer, from Washington University and Michigan University respectively. They analyze if firms should make that their staff sleep enough.

Spreitzer believes that, in the instance of Wahlberg, he is just moving his waking hours to a different (but extreme) time, and that he is likely to be more productive.

"There are certain advantages: you develop a discipline where you have a lot more time to meet yourself - to achieve your own goals before the family rises and the colleagues want to see you," she explains.

But going to bed at an early stage could lead to "sacrificing your social network and developing strong social interactions" that are required for healthy mental health.

"I guess you lose a lot of lovely dinner chats with the family where you're not sleeping or social events with friends when you go to your bed at 7.30 a.m.," she says.

Could it be a particularly early bird in your blood, however?

Owls and Larks

People and their sleep patterns are driven by circadian patterns — that is, 24-hour internal clocks, which regularly stimulate alertness and tiredness. Many tend to wake up and desire to get to bed every day at the same time – thus a shock can come to our bodies as we move time zones.

Based on these circadian patterns, the researcher's group persons into two main groups: larks and owls (late risers and sleepers).

Barnes argues that there is some natural difference between people, but that many of us tend to be larks as kids, turn to owls as teens and turn back to larkhood as we become older.

But he thinks that the amount of people who may be "super larks" who get up naturally, like Mark Wahlberg, at 2:30 am, is quite unusual.

One study indicates that night owls have an energy peak that arrives naturally in the evening and they feel rejuvenated and ready to take action. It's horrible for their sleep but fantastic for their productivity, which they don't have in the early stages.

Whenever I hear about the benefits of being an early bird, and how you get to get up with the sun (and the birds) so that I can succeed. I am an owl for the night—My best and most productive time starts when you nod your normal early riser.

Why resist nature? Why fight nature? After all, investigations have shown that we have been born night owls like that - genetic and biological. So here are 11 wonderful reasons for all of you owls to embrace late-night productivity habits, believe your inner clock, and disregard all the external societal expectations.

1. Peace and calm are found

Even on those days when I get up early, I get a lot more done in the night than at any other time of my day. I am not bombarded by queries, e-mails, texts, telephone calls or social media, and can concentrate on endlessly for hours.

2. You're more than likely a workhorse

A study in Belgium at the University of Liege discovered that owls stay intellectually aware far longer than their early counterparts for a long time after rising.

3. You always have a good time

Night owls can say yes to a social life at night since they know they're still going to have a few hours' productive time before they need to sleep once they come home.

4. You will be more enterprising

According to the University of Chicago, night owls are more likely to take a risk and to become successful entrepreneurs.

5. Probably you're stronger

Studies have demonstrated that the night owls have increased excitability of the motor cortex and spinal cord late at night. This is another strong justification for bucking tradition again and practising at night rather than in the morning. If you're like me, mornings aren't the time to bench your head with a huge weight.

6. You're free as a bird.

No conventions or meetings are arranged in the middle of the night, so you can work and play and work with more flexibility.

7. You will be more creative

Researchers at Milan university noticed a boost in innovation among night owls, noting that they tend to find answers outside the shops rather than their early bird counterparts.

8. You tend to be lot easier

Early risers often have higher stress hormone cortisol levels, and these elevated levels remain throughout the day, according to British researchers. This does not apply to owls at night. You don't receive the same level of cortisol injection early in the morning and remain relatively calm all day.

9. You can only have a higher IQ

Researcher Satoshi Kanazawa observed that extremely smart children tend to become nightly adults, who like to sleep seven days a week and to stay up late at night. Another study at the University of Madrid showed those night owls were more intelligent than early birds and made even greater salaries.

10. On the World Wide Web you may catch up

The night owls catch a quiet, calm internet if the early bird catches the worm. You can catch all the latest news and articles without the need to update dozens of other updates concurrently or to continually check for additional updates.

11. You can adjust to 9 to 5 (if you absolutely have to)

If night owls could always follow their biological desire to stay late, everything in their world would be great. The reality is that many owls of the night have a job to do during the early-bird hours. The good news is that owls at night may wake up much easier in the early morning than early risers, who often find it exceedingly difficult to spend their customary bedtime and stay up later.

CHAPTER 5:

Inspired by the quieter hours of the day

It has been claimed that early birds receive the worm, but equally night owls gain a great deal by being who they are. And now is the time for them to get some praise.

Please don't get us wrong: we are sleep advocates. And you must obtain the correct amount of sleep every day (7 to 9 hours for the normal adult) to stay healthy. This doesn't allow you to stay up late and go to sleep. But you could feel motivated to stay up a little later if your lifestyle allows a later wake time.

While a start of 2:30 am suggests a very long day and almost any sleep, Wahlberg's early bedtime indicates that he works every night for seven hours.

This is important to productivity — your health and cognitive abilities are affected by a lack of sleep.

Two American researchers from the University of Washington and University of Michigan, Christopher Barnes and Gretchen Spreitzer respectively, have examined this topic extensively. They analyze whether firms should ensure that their staff sleep adequately.

Spreitzer argues that his waking time in Wahlberg's instance is merely moving to a different (but extreme) starting time and that he is probably more productive.

"There are certain benefits: you are creating discipline in which you have a lot more time - to achieve your own goals before your family comes up before the coworkers want to meet you," she explains.

But bed early can lead to "sacrificing its social network and developing strong social interactions" that are important for optimal mental health.

"When you go to bed at 7:30, I guess you miss out on a lot of beautiful suppers with your family where you are not sleeping or social activities with friends," she says.

However, might it be a really early bird in your blood?

Owls and larks

Human beings and sleep patterns are guided by circadian patterns, that is to say, 24-hour internal clocks which regularly stimulate alertness and sleepiness. Many tend to wake and want to go to bed each day at the same time - this is why jet lags may make our bodies so shocks as we travel time zones.

Based on these circadian cycles, investigators are grouped into two large groups: larks and owls (late risers and sleepers).

Barnes adds that the population changes naturally, but many of us tend as youngsters to be larks, turn to owls as teens, and as we grow older, turn back to larkhood.

However, he estimates that the number of people out there who may be "super larks," who wake up naturally around 2:30 pm as Mark Wahlberg is quite unusual.

According to one study, night owls have an energy peak that arrives naturally in the evening and feels rejuvenated and ready to perform. It is negative for your sleeping behaviour, but absolutely fantastic for your productivity, which your early growing peers do not have.

Every time I hear all the advantages of being an early bird, and how to get up with the sun (and the birds), to succeed, it causes me to grind. I'm an owl of the night—the most productive time starts when your average early rise nods away.

Why resist nature? Why fight nature? After all, investigations have shown that we have born night owls like that - genetic and biological. So for all of your night owls, here are 11 good reasons for adopting your late-night productivity habits, trusting your internal clock and ignoring all those external societal pressures.

1. You will find peace

I get much more done at night, even on those days when I get up early than at any other time. I am not plagued with queries, emails, texts, phone calls and social media and can focus on endlessly for hours.

2. You're more than likely a workhorse

A study at the University of Liege, Belgium, discovered that owls stay intellectually alert significantly longer than their early bird counterparts for a long time after waking.

3. You will always have a happy hour

Night owls can and can say yes to a sociable night life since they know they're still going to have hours of production before they have to sleep when they return home.

4. You will be entrepreneurial more likely.

Night owls have a higher risk-taking propensity, according to the University of Chicago, and can become successful entrepreneurs.

5. Probably you're stronger

Studies demonstrate that night owls show an increase in late-night hours of the motor cortex and spinal cord excitation. This is another solid reason to practice bucking tradition and not in the morning at night. If you're like me, the morning isn't the time to bench your head with a crazy amount of weight.

6. You're free as a bird.

Terms or meetings are not planned in the middle of the night, so you are free to work and play and work, allowing a lot of flexibility.

7. You will be more creative

Researchers at a university in Milan saw an upsurge in creativity amongst the night owls and that they are far more likely than their early bird counterparts to come up with external solutions.

8. You tend to be lot easier

Early risers have typically higher amounts of the stress hormone cortisol, and these elevated levels stay throughout the day, British researchers say. This is not the case for owls at night. You do not receive the same level of cortisol injection early in the morning and you stay relative calm all day.

9. You can have a higher IQ only

Researcher Satoshi Kanazawa has shown that very smart children are often night adults who prefer to stay late at night and sleep seven days a week. Another study at Madrid University indicated those night owls tested more generally and earned even higher wages than early birds.

10. On the World Wide Web, you may catch up

If the early bird takes the worm, the night owls will catch a calm, quiet Internet. You have an opportunity to review all the latest news and articles without the need to concurrently catch dozens or check back for more updates regularly.

11. You can adapt to a 9 to 5 (if you absolutely have to)

If night owls could always follow their biological need to stay late, all in their world would be great. The fact is that many owls throughout the night have a job that needs them to work during the early-bird hours. The good news is that night owls find it simpler to wake up early and be productive compared to early risers who often find it exceedingly hard to spend their normal sleeping hour and stay up later.

"A calm setting is a therapeutic place"

In current technological culture, ceaseless exposure to auditory stimuli is part of everyday existence. Amid the roar of automobiles, trains and aircraft, the noise of construction and digital equipment, silence appears to have become a luxury. Cultivating silence may nevertheless have some overlooked advantages that can cover professional life.

There is a vast range of sounds in all kinds of places every day, and most people seem to be adapted to continual noise exposures. In any imaginable public area, popular music or radio chatting resonates and it is now uncommon to get inside the house without listening to a television show in the background even if the residents genuinely do not watch it. These established habits create the illusion of a silence-friendly culture.

Paradoxically, silence seems to be very much sought after. Noise cancellation headphones are marketed for hundreds of dollars and individuals are retreating more and more in pricey silence.

In 2011, a large marketing effort was even conducted by the Finnish Tourism Board in silence. The purpose of this marketing was to make people to Finland experience the 'beauty of the silent earth' and 'take the sound of stillness.' Marketing specialists have created a series of photographs with the title "Silence, please."

The use of silence as a marketing approach shows a greater appreciation of stillness, and many people may be overwhelmed by repeated exposure to loudness.

Harmful Noise and Workers

Every year, 30 million people are exposed to harmful levels of noise at work in the United States. As a result, thousands of them suffer hearing loss.

Constant loud sound exposure might generate stress and decrease productivity. Focus and communication are also affected. High noise levels might potentially cause accidents or injuries by making it difficult to hear warning signals.

A study carried out by experts at the University of California, Irvine, has shown that a typical officer is only given an average of 11 minutes from each interruption and it takes about 25 minutes after an unplanned interruption to return to the original duty. These estimates show how uncontrolled interactions in open workspaces diminish productivity.

A noisy working environment can also influence the performance of employees indirectly by affecting their health.

Constant noise exposure was connected with the body's major stress hormone, high levels of cortisol. Like strong light, noise is a signal to the body that something is happening for which it must be awake. This form of stress causes the creation of cortisol, which increases blood pressure and blood sugar.

These modifications assist people to endure short stress periods, but they can cause substantial harm if they are repeatedly triggered by stressors like a steady sound. Chronically high levels of cortisol have been connected with blood pressure, heart disease, resistance to insulin, obesity and diabetes type 2.

A Cornell University study on office noise indicated that workers working in loud conditions might adapt their workstations ergonomically for comfort, which can contribute to physical difficulties. Exposure to continuous disturbance can also affect the quality of sleep by interrupting circadian rhythms.

Low health can damage the performance of an employee, and many people are not at their best in bustling, noisy jobs.

Some people don't appreciate a silent environment and are lonely and alone. Many claims to work with music or background noise more productive. It is also an excellent inducement for certain individuals to communicate with colleagues as needed.

Five Quiet Time benefits

Recent research offers five tangible benefits of taking time to remain silent.

1. Silence Cuts Stress

Silence first emerged as a baseline or control in the scientific study against which scientists measure the effects of noise. Researchers have often accidentally examined it. In a 2006 research on the impacts on sound, Luciano Bernardi examined the effectiveness of music in the modulation of stress.

The silence was employed as a control between various music clips. These small moments of quiet proved to be more brain soothing than so-called "relaxing" music. Bernardi feels that the contrast with noise increases this relaxing impact of stillness.

It can thus be hypothesized that momentary quiet in contrast to other sounds can aid people to cope with stress. Getting out for a few minutes to a quiet location in the workplace as you feel overwhelmed could be a smart method to relieve stress and boost performance.

Medical experts are increasingly using quiet as a means of reducing stress. Many doctors now recommend meditation practice to anxiety-related patients. This practice is to remain silent and tranquil while focusing on a certain thought, object or image to develop an awareness of the present moment and achieve an emotionally calm and clear state of mind.

2. Silence enhances cognitive functionality.

A 2013 study by the National Library of Medicine shows that long-term silence exposure can trigger the brain to generate new cells. Imke Kirste, a Duke University researcher, has been investigating the impact of noise and stillness on mice's brains.

The stillness was designed to be a control in the study, but Kirste found that when mice were exposed to two hours of silence every day, new cells were being created at the hippocampus, the memory and learning brain zone.

The creation of new brain cells does not necessarily lead to concrete cognitive advantages. In this case, though, the cells seemed to become neurons.

Taking time for silence every day could enable you to keep up your ability to learn and store new things, which can make your professional life a lot easier.

3. Silence enhances creativity

The ability to shut the outer world off can increase opportunities for fresh ideas.

The psychologist Jonathan Smallwood concluded in a 2013 study of literature on cognitive and clinical psychology that human creativity mostly depends on one's ability to disengage from the external environment and concentrate on self-generated thinking.

Self-produced thinking is characterized by internal mental activity, which occurs while the mind is not engaged with the external environment. This includes daydreaming, pondering about the future and wandering the mind. We can access internal thoughts, memories and ideas when we can disengage and relax.

Neuroimaging research has revealed the default brain network as the primary source of self-generated thinking. Increasing evidence reveals that the default network plays a key role in creative thought. In reality, multiple studies in brain imaging show activating default areas in creative problem resolution and artistic performance.

4. Silence improves your mood

When the brain is unrelated to external inputs it helps you to recognize and examine your emotional condition. Reflecting on how you feel can enable you to better tackle problems, which can improve your mind tremendously.

The use of the default brain network also enables you to focus on the current situation, which decreases negative thinking and worry.

Working and being interrupted in a constantly noisy atmosphere can be frustrating. Breaking away from this hectic atmosphere and retreating a few minutes into a peaceful spot can make your day more pleasant.

It could be a good idea to switch off social media notifications on your phone and computer to limit interruptions and sensory input.

You can also let your employees know exactly when you are available for discussion and tell them that you do not want to disrupt your work at particular times.

5. Silence helps you concentrate

In everyday life, especially at employment, the brain gets sensory data continuously. The media's prefrontal cortex, which is engaged in focus, problem-solving, and high-order thinking, has an important burden.

Constant inputs can overwhelm this brain area. As a result, you may grow tired and struggle to concentrate. Fewer distractions allow the brain to concentrate. Several studies have revealed that in quiet circumstances the brain can replenish its attention resources.

The theory of attention restoration, drawn out by psychologists Rachel and Stephen Kaplan in 1989, shows that exposure to silent natural environments promotes a more effortless cognitive performance that allows the brain to release its sensory guard and to refill its capacities.

While escape to natural space during working hours is not always possible, going outside at a peaceful point of the day might assist you to regain the ability to concentrate on your activities.

That is why nighttime stops and allows you to accomplish a more productive job.

Bored?

Bored and unable to sleep at night is a prominent symptom of this.

CHAPTER 6:

Are the hours dragging past without purpose?

This is the real kicker for most night owls

Many people with insomnia have a common complaint: "At night I can't turn my mind off." When sleep is a fleeting wish in the quietness of the night, the mind seems to churn and to foster alertness in some.

What causes night-time racing thoughts and how may they be relieved? Learn more about ways to soothe your mind, how racing thinking may be reduced and stress or anxiety minimized and how insomnia can be resolved using effective relaxation techniques.

Racing Thoughts and Insomnia Causes

In any case, insomnia may occur in the correct circumstances. During situations of stress or anxiety, it may be difficult to fall or sleep.

Sleep is better when stress and stressors don't flood our thoughts. These concerns activate and make it difficult to sleep. This may appear to be something beyond your control, but it's not.

Racing thoughts can manifest themselves in several ways. Some people describe this as a film that plays in your mind at night, pictures flash in your consciousness while you lie waking with your eyes closed.

It is sometimes experienced as a rumour.

To comprehend rumination, envision a cow that chews his cud slowly and persistently—food from his belly is replenished and swallowed. If it's not taken care of correctly, it comes back.

Similarly, stress or anxiety sources can emerge to your mind to be reviewed, rehabilitated and reworked. Maybe there is no obvious remedy, and after being briefly suppressed, it comes back in front of your thoughts, especially during calm hours at night.

Although racing thinking may exclusively occur among people with anxiety problems, this is not necessarily the case. Again, stress can contribute to its incidence even among persons who don't identify themselves as anxious or even anxious.

This can be heightened in times of severe stress: job loss, divorce, movements or deprivation after a loved one's death. The content of these thoughts can pertain to work, finances, family, relationships, health or other stressors.

Regardless, these thoughts can be quite disruptive and need to be deliberately changed to resolve them.

How to ease the thinking of racing

You have to refuse the fuel to start spinning into the dark, to turn a racing mind off. This can be achieved by reducing stress, spending some time in bed relaxation and distraction and relaxation.

Setting aside some time during the day to address your stressors might be quite helpful. Sometimes this is dubbed "planned time for concern."

Take some time every day to identify, list and work on the reasons for stress, anxiety or tension. This can be done by spending time writing or reviewing a list of things that contribute to stress in your life each day.

Write them down. Write them down. Then, in a second column, suggest some actions to address and alleviate the stress.

How to use 'Planed Time of Work'

For instance, if you have a large project in two weeks' work, this may cause you to experience heightened stress. It may seem overwhelming. There is no way you can accomplish it all. You even don't know where to start. This stress can be disabling.

Instead of getting overwhelmed, break it into handy pieces – and then work. Make the following things in the action plan: examine the files, speak to your colleague, set a meeting, compose the proposal and conclude the presentation.

When you do the duties day after day, you cross them off. The stressor itself can eventually be eliminated from the list.

Some items on the list may not have a clear resolution. This can generate more anxiety and deplete your energy all day long. Tell yourself you must let go of it. Tomorrow, come back to it.

Maybe things will change and by that time you will have a plan to help you go ahead. In the meantime, concentrate your attention on things you can change.

By writing out your stressors, you put your stress sources a name. It also helps you to get them out of your mind. You don't have to think about them or remember them all the time so you don't forget.

You will uncover ways to relieve stress by making an action plan. When you take up your chores and examine them every day, you cannot overcome the problem with a sense of fulfilment.

If thoughts concerning stress are present at night, you simply say to yourself, I don't have to think about it right now. Tomorrow, I'll ponder about it during my regular time of concern. Then I can address it. It can shut down the stream of thoughts and enable you to (or return to) sleep.

Downhill before bedtime

It can be helpful to relax before bed to make the night a relaxing time.

Put your work aside. Turn the computer off. Stay away from the phone and social media, such as Facebook and Twitter. There will always be more to accomplish, but today you have done enough. Now is the time to relax and get ready for sleep.

Durate at least 30 minutes, perhaps one or two hours, before bedtime and relax.

Complete the time with relaxation. You may want to read, hear music, watch TV, stretch, shower or bath, meditate or pray. Ease the night by relaxing before you try to sleep.

During your bedtime, or when you're up at night, you might wish to include some extra relaxing practices. This could include breathing, gradual muscle relaxation or guided imaging.

These activities will distract you from sleep effort, lessen racing thinking and assist you in sleep. These simple strategies are available in books or other internet sites.

You can turn your mind off at night. It will make it easier for you to sleep in the night if you allow time to deal with stress during the day and spend time relaxing before bedtime. The use of distracting relaxation techniques can aid in the night.

You can do this. You can. Reduce your thinking and put your sleeplessness to sleep for good.

Speak to your doctor about alternative treatment choices, including cognitive insomnia treatment (CBTI) and medicines to reduce anxiety or insomnia drugs. Our below Doctor's Guide might help you start the conversation.

CHAPTER 7:

Don't just survive the night, learn to thrive and *become a hunter.*

Do you not enjoy the idea of waking up to work too early in the morning? Well, even though somebody who wants to achieve a lot in one day is fairly advantageous, not everyone's good. Most often, for one cause or another, you will sleep late so it becomes harder for you to wake up early in the morning.

The good news is that you can always be a night owl. You can do it as the owls do, converting your day tonight. In addition, night owl stereotypes were extremely productive in comparison to early risers. Unfortunately, working at night is never easy much like waking up early in the morning. You have to use it.

Luckily, unlike an early riser, if you love to sleep late, you only need to make a few tweaks. I prepared for you in this article some ideas and tactics on how to become a very productive owl at night.

Turn your bedroom into a sleeping atmosphere

If you plan to sleep late to work on your harder tasks, your sleep pattern must be changed. It is normally suggested that you sleep every night for seven to eight hours. You must wake at 10 am if you want to work until late and sleep at 3 a.m.

But how do you transform your bedroom into a refuge for sleeping? Just keep the lights out, simple. You make it easier to switch off the lights and use dark transparent curtains to hide your windows. You must also do away with noise. Switch off your music system and make sure your door and walls are soundproof that noises remain outside.

When to drink your coffee cup

Coffee is the best treatment for individuals who want to be awake. Just like drinking a cup of coffee at night will keep you alert and focused on your work all night long, taking it in the morning can make the remainder of your day more vibrant.

But when are you supposed to take it? How much are you supposed to take? That's where it gets tough. You may be tempted to eat more cups of coffee when you work during the night to keep the cold. Don't do this. Don't do this. Coffee can keep you awake for around 6 to 8 hours, so if you do, let's say at 3:00 a.m, after 8 hours, which is 11 night, you would be unable to sleep.

Avoid sleeping habits.

Sleepover may destroy your night hours, just as waking up late in the morning. When you sleep too much, your body will become accustomed to long sleep times, so that even when it is not right, you will fall asleep. It's a waste of time and money, in addition. Keep to a certain number of hours.

In our instance, it is important to sleep at least seven to eight hours for a person who plans to work late. You will have to sleep earlier if you have additional sleep issues, such as sleep apnea. You should also avoid other harmful sleep habits, such as taking frequent sleep drugs, forcing you to sleep and more.

Don't squander your hours of the night doing nothing

You sleep late so you could do a bit of work, right? Why spend precious time on Twitter and Facebook when a deadline approaches? Moreover, you attempt to be a very productive night owl, and that's what converted your days into nights. You must stay focused on your tasks to boost your productivity, except when it's a weekday or a vacation and you have nothing to do.

Choose a job that promotes your path

You can't be a night owl if you have to report to your job before 8 a.m. the following day. You must adapt to becoming an early bird. Some organizations in today's environment where technology rules favour night shifts. There are also such groups that establish a goal for you after some time. You can choose the night shift if your job supports night and day shifts. When it comes to hitting targets, find out whether you can complete your work at home to work on it at night.

Avoid many tasks

Multitasking is one thing that makes working late a problem. Remember that the fact that your day is overnight might not be used by your brain.

Even if you had a coffee cup, you're still going to feel dizzy. When you feel sleepy, the final thing that you want to do is work on more than one assignment. In addition, the quality of your work is compromised. Try to concentrate on one thing at a time.

Avoid eating late in the night

Many night workers are often tempted to eat late in the night. Keep in mind that you could eat too much of your fourth meal, which also doesn't make a better idea if you want to keep yourself healthy. Furthermore, eating at night will encourage sleep in your workspace.

Exercise

Exercise, a few hours a day, is best known for night owls. You can't do it the way early birds do it, however. You will need a special living routine. Take an example; at 3 am are you planning to sleep and awaken at 10 am. Most experts advise you to exercise before 8 am or after 5 pm. Night Owls ideally should be finding alternative slots to accommodate their needs. You can try to find out if there is a 24-hour fitness centre around your area or create a fitness centre like a treadmill and a few weights.

Waking up early in the morning is a terrific idea for a person who wants to do a lot in one day. Unfortunately, especially for a person who loves sleeping late, it is never easy. The good news is that you can decide to be an owl for the night, which means your days will be transformed into evening work. But to achieve a lot in one night, you must use several recommendations above and find a job that accepts the night owl approach. Or even better, be your boss!

CHAPTER 8:

Being a Night Owl is resilient, empowering and rewarding

The regular 9-to-5 working day can be excruciating for night owls and early birds. Every morning the fatigued night owl drags itself blindly into the office, while the early hip bird discovers that its vigour is diminishing even before leaving the time.

But there are ways to deal with it. These survival methods for folks with body clocks out of sync with their employers' hours are offered by experts.

Recognize that nature is not food

Early birds and owls of the night do not pick their way of life, nor should they blame for their corporal eccentricities. "That's a genetically determined physiological feature, such as tall or blonde," says Carolyn Schur, a Saskatchewan human resources consultant and author of Birds of a Different feather, Canadian-based Birds of a Different Feather: Talk about their characteristic behaviours: Early Birds and Night Owls. A night owl with trouble working on time is not lazy, and an early bird who cannot work too late in the day doesn't slack.

"Do not always try and apologize for your lifestyle," said Schur, noting that up to 40 percent of the population may be predisposed to early birds and night ovens. Further research shows that approximately 10 percent of the population is "extreme" owls, or early birds, which may become chronically tired, unwell or sad if they work against their nature in a timetable.

Enabling Yourself

If your body rebels, do not submit yourself to working 9 to 5. If your organization has no flexible planning policy already, approach your boss. Explain how working your favourite hours can improve productivity and efficiency for example or, if you arrive early or stay late, how your employer can extend your hours of service to no extra cost. "For your employer, frame your request in terms that signify something," Schur says.

Bear in mind

If your boss allows you to start late or leave early, you must still be a team player. "Do not let your colleagues hang up, waiting for a work they could rely on," says Keirsten Moore, PhD, Associate Dean at Columbus School of Management, University of Capital, Ohio. Keep track of the deadlines and tell your employees and managers explicitly how to reach you if you aren't in the office during regular business hours, says Moore.

Recognize yourself

Moore says it's one of the main hurdles to working varied hours to overcome the notion that you are not focused or effective. "The challenge is to make it evident that you contribute your entire weight," she says. In the best-case situation, your boss's night habits or early bird trends are reflective. However, if they do not, you may have to take additional actions to be visible.

For example, when you complete your early-morning or late-night work, use email or voice mail with time and date stamps. Hand-pack projects to make it evident when you were at the office. When you arrive early, park near where usually your boss parks so he'll be aware of your early arrival.

Make acceptance

Do not consider your schedule set in stone if you come to work late or depart early. Be flexible enough to attend the 8 a.m. or after-hours brainstorming session occasionally. Although the time of day may not be ideal for you, you can raise it with sufficient warning. "The owl of the night must prepare for what he is going to say or contribute to the morning night session and the early bird must prepare for the late afternoon session that morning," Schur says. "At your best time of the day, you must put your best work on paper."

Find the right economy

In many firms and industries, flexible scheduling is simply not an option. If your happiness or your health is vital, find better work, says Schur. In general, early birds work better in 8-to-5 employment than night owls, but would suffer from working evenings or night shifts, she notes. Night owls are drawn to work in the service and entertainment sector during the late afternoon, at night and overnight.

CHAPTER 9:

Breakthrough Ideas

Thanks to circadian rhythm, at various times of the day your body feels more awake or dormant. The phenomena are normal and not everybody's rhythm — some people are filled with pep at 7:00 AM (they would be the early birds) while others are fed up at 11:00 AM (night owls). But what if you wish to move from one to the next? Maybe your new job requires early hours or your kids have sports before school. Turning from a night owl to an early bird needs to change your circadian rhythm that is easy to achieve.

1. First adjust the morning. One of the reasons owls stay so late at night is that they are not tired. You have to make sure you fall asleep earlier in the lot and you have to wake up much sooner than usual. It will be tough for a couple of days as you adjust, but be consistent: After several days of setting your alarm at 6:00 a.m., you will be tired if 10:00 a.m. rolls around.

2. Go slow. Go slow. If a wakeup at 6:00 AM is too much to ease after years of increase at 7:30 AM, be easy. Start by shifting your

alarm forward each morning in 15 minutes over of a week, until you reach your new time.

3. Have a bright morning, even if it is dark at 6:00 AM, it is incredibly tough to feel energetic. If the summer is over, throw the shades open. If not, turn some lamps on. The light will reduce the sleep-inducing melatonin produced in your body and make you feel more alert. And don't hit snooze whatever you do!

4. Bump up your schedule for the night. If you want your schedule, change the time you spend your normal activities—whether it's eating to the gym, supper, watching TV or mingling with friends—an hour or so earlier. If your schedule doesn't allow it, consider shortening or alternative days of activity to help move your bedtime to an equivalent number of minutes for a new wake up time.

5. Stay steady. Stay steady. The fastest approach to get a new schedule for your body is to stay on weekends. Your body benefits from going to bed and waking up every day at the same time — you don't have to work even on days or the kids to school. Sleeping in at the moment may feel fine, but you will most likely find it more difficult to get to bed early on Sunday to make one rough on Monday morning.

CHAPTER 10:

Deliberate Innovating.

Companies typically label people for maintaining specific schedules, but it is sometimes unfair. Consider the term 'night owl,' which usually involves staying late—maybe a binge-watch TV.

The association usually suggests a person is not productive even when he is reading or cleaning during the late hours. But it doesn't work any longer in our modern economy, connected by technology and packed with creative hours.

Consider differently — and selfishly — in your time

"I have to rule the clock, not be ruled by it." Golda Meir Gold

The thing is, everybody has a distinct engine and a different measure of when they are most productive. Working all or part of the time remotely may imply unorthodox hours, including weekends, which is becoming a new normal.

People who suggest you shouldn't work on a Saturday - because it's the weekend — don't care about your objectives and dreams. These people will most likely come home from their work and spend the remainder of the night watching television. You are the type of night owl who burns the midnight oil to make your aspirations and goals.

You are fighting the crowd — the wind

You are a businessman, thus you're a self-motivated and goal-driven person. You haven't been an entrepreneur to go and get out of a dead-end job and then rinse and repeat from Monday to Friday.

Learn the most productive hours of your day. When you work between 12 am and 2 am (and work from home or can get you to work that time) you find yourself most concentrated, then do it by any means! If you prefer to work a little each day, if your work-life balance means, then do it more at night.

Redefine the phrase "night owl" and disregard these labels and judgments.

CHAPTER 11:

How about that Side Hustle that every morning person put you down on?

There are so many fantastic ways these days to earn extra money on the side. You may find many options and advice to help you get started by just conducting an online search.

There is, however, one big difficulty that people neglect to address. You require a lot of time and energy to hustle efficiently. If you strive to pay off your debt, save more, improve your revenue to invest more or achieve any other goal, you're going to want your side bump to be sustainable and not exhausting.

If it's not, you're going to find yourself burning out too fast. I worked 15 to 20 hours a week in my day job over 40 hours a week in the highest of my side hustle and bustle experience. I might have burned out repeatedly, but I have been finding ways to optimize my time and energy to keep earning more money.

Have you found a side hustle, but you just have to find the time and energy to get started? These tips are there to aid you.

GET ORGANIZED

When you start hustling, the first thing you want to do is organize yourself. You may prioritize your time and energy in this way. It is important to know exactly what you have to do and when.

Determine when you are most productive and commit your time to side-hustle work. You can also use a planner to keep track of your daily to-do list.

Don't forget to plan unpaid work and determine how successfully you will accomplish it. This might take the time to promote your services, reply to emails, take the time to transport to your side-hustle or even deliver invoices if you are freelance.

VALUE YOUR TIME LIKE AN INVESTMENT

We all spend time somehow. If you hustle side by side, your goal should be to free as much time as feasible. You will therefore have to leave out certain activities that can impair your success.

Watching too much television is usually the first thing to do. If you watch TV for two hours every night, you can free up to 10 hours on weekdays. You will still gain 5 hours even if you cut that time in half.

You may also wish to spend time on social media doing nothing or spending time playing games.

You can also start preparing food for the week to save the time you spend on supper or laundry services.

If you read web articles during your lunch break, instead try working on your side turmoil.

Find out some of the tasks in your life which occupy a lot of time. Then see which can be streamlined or eliminated. You can have more time to hustle and drink.

OWN IT

I always advise either side hustlers, because you can't choose both normally. You presumably are either a person in the morning or the night.

I'm a person in the morning. When I just want to relax and spend time with my family, I can't think to do anything very useful at night.

I decided to get up at 5 am most morning to do more work when I hurried side by side. Some may sound strange, but if you would prefer to sleep in and stay on the bustling side later in the evening, you can do so. If you have chosen one or the other, it should match your productivity levels so that you can complete even more work.

I know a few people who can do a ton of work in night and that's right for them. Find out what works for you.

KNOW THE TIME TO REST

To add to my final remark, I would not suggest that anyone shorten their sleep hours significantly. Every night you require an average of at least 7-8 hours of sleep. This is vital if your regular job and your side hustle span a ton of hours.

I know that I become grumpy and inefficient at work that wastes more time when I do not have enough sleep at night.

If you follow several of the above guidelines, you should know when it's time to stop for a night and rest so you can be ready for the following day. You can always finish what you do the next day.

Do you work?

Nothing feels worse than leaving a job, you feel tired about working another job. Because you spend so much time working, you may be just as fond of your side business because you spend a good number of hours there.

Moreover, you have to recognize that the kind of work you do can substantially influence the energy and motivation you need to do. If your workday isn't as creative as you would want, try a creative side-job like an outlet.

Determine what your skills are and what kind of work you would really like to accomplish. Choosing a side turmoil that thrills you and makes you good might make all the difference in creating time and energy to work on it. Moreover, it can be helpful for your health too.

CHAPTER 12:

You are a night owl, and soon to be a creature of successful habit

Why we work better at night?

You will have to work on environmental factors with your work unless you live in a soundproof cage, where food is served to you three times a day. Kids, merchants, spouses, friends: we all have fun things, or just required tasks in our lives.

E.B. White famously observed, "A writer who awaits ideal work conditions is going to die without putting a word on paper."

But wait till night, and all these distractions are gone. The dog was walked, the people were in bed, and there was no more telephone, text or email.

Most night owls were born in that way but certain of them are adapted to become a night owl, as did Morgan St. James, writer of seventeen books including the award-winning 'Incest, Murder and a Miracle.'

"I've never been a night owl until I've become a novelist. In my opinion, my high level of creativity seems to take off at aroun11 pmpm and I often work on my novels till 2 or 3 a.m. I believe this is so because, although I write throughout the day, as a full-time writer, I spend promotional time, make transcripts, attend workshops and other essential duties during the day. Then my mind is clear and tranquil after some night of relaxation. I turn on classical piano music and let my mind explore. For me, I do not establish words or time restrictions or maximums. I will continue to write until I'm ready to stop."

The founder of Royale Studios digital agency Óscar Mota Mangandi agrees that many creators prefer to work at night:

"Working at night is more productive for things and IT professionals, because you get fewer distractions, people don't disturb you, callers aren't there, mail entry doesn't happen, social media notifications and so on. You can concentrate on what you need to do (open offices are a real nightmare to be productive in).

I did this for 15 years, but now I have to take care of a young baby (1yr old). It makes my schedule a little harder, since I have to wait for her to sleep before I can start my night ritual. I've gone a few hours to accomplish my job but I'm still incredibly productive.

My routine will begin at 9 am, then during the day I will have a siesta and continue working till 3 am."

They're not alone as creatives who work best at night. Everything went best in the work for Bob Dylan, Franz Kafka and Marcel Proust; and novelist Thomas Wolfe did not even put putting his style on paper before midnight each night, prepared with abundant cups of coffee.

At Mornings, we are not just bad: we are done that way

Hedonism: a person who is devoted to the pursuit of pleasure

In general, night owls envy people to wake up and to feel wake instantaneously. People who can do a whole day's work 10 am to 10pm. We have often tried to drive our body into a new pattern – we would have done it if we could manage it for thirty days.

New research demonstrates that it is not only almost impossible but it is really harmful to our health. Slightly counter-intuitive, since other research revealed a reduced life span for night owls. Should we not aim to get into 'healthy habits'?

Studies have found that those night owls are more susceptible to despair, anxiety and drug usage. If one looks at the list of writers and designers who are owls at night, this is difficult to argue. "Anxiety is the handmaid of creation," stated T.S Eliot.

That being said, it makes sense to stay at least relatively near to Mother Nature's chrono-type if we want to be productive: rather than being sleep-deprived through the day, lay awake throughout the night.

Founder and CEO of two firms, Casey Gardonio-Foat, Casey York Design, which manufactures luxury home-decor goods, and Wink & Rise, the online retailer for things that make and enjoy sleep, were relieved if scientism enabled her to take on her night owl habits.

"I have had night owl trends since my young years and have just been relieved to find out that research validates the existence of many chronotypes. Now, instead of feeling guilty of sleeping when all my home is productive hours, I can embrace and enjoy the productivity and momentum I feel work late in the night.

However, I think that the reason I can accomplish this is that I'm committed to sleeping 7 to 8 hours each 24 hours—even owls have to sleep. As a self-employed person, I am lucky to be able to stay up late and sleep when I have to, and when needed, I supplement my night sleep with nappies at night. A normal night for me may be work at 9 pm (after my children go to bed) and work around 2 or 3 am till 8 a.m.; a nap of 90 minutes around four o'clock may follow.

By ensuring I have enough rest, I can be alert and productive in my wakeful hours and do more than if I find to adjust my body to the early waking and the early evening.'

Night owls were accepted in 2012 when Kathryn Schultz, a writer in New York, released an essay on her life as someone who seldom sleeps.

There is an air of hedonism that stays all night. Of prudence, and joy of life. Even if genetics: perhaps hedonism comes with these DNA strands?

When the world goes to sleep, it is easier to be productive

At Timing, we are great advocates of friction and distractions removal and of using every tool in your arsenal to manage time and stress. If it means waiting till you'll have gone to sleep the rest of the world (or at least those in your time zone!), so be it!

This is particularly true for entrepreneurs with families, even though they did not usually work late. No distractions or other calls allow you room to concentrate because Sireesha, a remote worker and founder of the Crowdworknews.com has discovered: "Working for late nights is because I have a calm, serene time. Children have gone to bed, my brain still works faster, and this time I'm up to my unfinished day's tasks.

I am an early riser, but most of my mornings are about checking emails, speaking with my freelancer, etc. There is hence a higher chunk of 'business work' at night.

For over 8 years, I've been in my remote job and manage my online business for two years. Working remotely or without a typical office means working at any time. To do the most work, becoming an owl for the night is my way. In just two years I couldn't have succeeded in generating a full-time wage if it wasn't for this arrangement."

However, you don't have to wake up early for an entire day's work. Nicole Faith, who has worked with entrepreneurs in 10caratcreations.com to build online services companies and founded the Digital Nomad Business Directory, nevertheless manages to be highly productive, although missing it altogether in the morning. "I personally feel more natural to be on a later schedule. I never liked that morning.

My routine looks like that:

Wake up from 11 am to 1 pm, unless I meet earlier. Eat breakfast, make my number one focus for a day (which can grow a part of a business, write a blog, do an interview, etc.) and then I accomplish other little tasks for my company.

I do not work more than 4-6 hours every day, but I spend a lot of time self-educating and self-improving. At night, I'm most creative, which is when I get a lot of fantastic ideas. I use the night as a springboard for insane ideas that I wouldn't else think of for my business and the companies that I develop for my customers.

I stay up late doing hobbies like reading, watching things or other work that keep my mind busy but not working. I am in my finest position when I give myself a rest from work.

Once I have an idea, I'm going to the races to implement it or investigate it more.

I've always been a night person and have been doing this for the last five years with my company.

As long as I get something important done every day (at the thing of my day), I'm productive."

If thoughts come greatest in the night, then accept them, don't fight them! While all the mood seems to wake up early, there are undoubtedly plenty of good, healthy, rich night owls. Jonah Peretti, CEO of Buzzfeed and co-founder of the Huffington Post, wakes at 8:30 a.m., whereas Mark Zuckerberg wakes up at 8 a.m. which sounds still early, until you know he often runs 60 hour weeks away and still has 3 hours more sleep than Branson.

When you plan to move to your natural biorhythm, have a look at a Mac productivity program like Timing to find out the hours in which you are most productive. The timing might also determine your work hours for you. The best work time applications take sleep patterns into account instead of capping your day at midnight. It can catch the worm from the early bird, but it is the night owl who succeeds in peace, quiet and creativity.

Screw, a morning person, we night animals know how to have fun and do it!

Night people also have a greater core body temperature in the afternoon, which could be a sign of heightened energy at the time, he added..."

"Types of the night" tend to wake up later in the morning.

If you're a night person, never change and turn to a morning person, you can be as productive as an early riser.

CHAPTER 13:

Life-changing habits, visions and unbreakable life goals.

Would you like to see a sunrise or count the stars of midnight? Are you creative and optimistic when you come out of bed in the morning, or when everybody else has gone to bed in the night? And what about it—would you like to look and feel more like Mary Poppins or Oscar the Grouch if you had to wake up at 6:00 am?

Your responses depend on your chronotype, a physiologically robust tendency for your body and brain to work best at specific times of the day. Most of you are in the middle—you don't like waking up for a run at 5 a.m., but after midnight you're not the one to buzz with energy either. But undoubtedly many of us have advanced or delayed chronotypes. We could, therefore, be extreme morning larks or owls of the night.

How can I have a reputation for the bathroom?

Personally, I am an owl of the night. Back in college I never signed up for classes before 10:00 a.m. and I could comfortably stay until 2:00 in the afternoon without diminishing my energy—that is, studying. And at college, there was no difficulty with that! I had no rounds 7 a.m. or 8 a.m. meetings, so I could blissfully live my body and brain on their schedule. But the more I get into my career the more my biology has to deal with the great awful world constructed by and for morning people.

NIGHT OWL COPING AND HEALTH

And it's not only a negative reputation problem. People suffering from late chronotype (i.e., night owls) are more likely to develop psychological illnesses, addiction, high blood pressure, obesity, type 2 diabetes, and even infertility. But it's not because owls are ill intrinsically. This is because we are compelled to live a life of misalignment – our biology does not meet our external expectations and this causes us to have less healthy clock-keeping habits. For example, I wager you sleep in on weekends if you are a delayed chronotype person. You try "to go to bed in a decent hour," but you can't help throwing and turning your iPad late in the night. Did you ever use sunglasses in the morning because you are not yet ready to seem human? These habits are perfectly understandable—I used to do them all.

Sadly, these customs regularly disturb your biological inner clock, called the circadian rhythm. This is no little matter since the circadian system maintains all your biological systems in schedule and works smoothly including your metabolism, hormonal secretion, cognitive function, muscular tone and even mood. If your body and mind are the Grand Central Station, all the clocks at the station are the circadian system. When the large clock tower always matches the times of train drivers, which also matches the times of every time and objects' watch, everything goes smoothly. But imagine that the time of that gigantic clock tower would change only randomly, and nobody could be certain they knew what time it was. Imagine this railway station's mayhem!

It is not surprising that shift workers, who have an even larger extreme circadian misalignment version, have greater health issues like as obesity than their non-shift working partners. Even frightening is that shifting is the sole non-chemical item in the carcinogenic list of the American Cancer Society, meaning experts believe that shifting work raises the risk of cancer for a work. Even if you are not a shift worker but even swing back and forth between your weekend sleep schedule and weekend schedule for several hours, you are at increased risk of weight gain, obesity, diabetes and depression.

CHAPTER 14:

Unlimited, Effortless Methods

Waking up at dawn can be easy for some, but those who want to go to bed later often fight.

Studies have indicated that evenings people—so-called "night owls"—may be at increased risk of certain health problems, especially if their sleep habits are interrupted or cut short by an internal body clock which commonly causes later than normal sleep and wakes time.

A study in "Sleep Medicine" published this week has revealed that late risers are not necessarily obliged to turn to drugs to regulate their body clocks – but can instead make simple changes to their sleep cycle.

Recent experiments have asked about 22 healthy people – who generally fall asleep at 2.30 a.m. and wake up at 10.15 a.m. – to advance their sleeping schedule to investigate if the circadian rhythm of a night owl can be shifted with simple, non-pharmacological adjustments.

The experiment, conducted by scientists of Surrey and Birmingham Universities in England and from Monash University in Australia, showed volunteers following a list of modest changes over three weeks:

- Wake up two to three hours before regular time to wake up
- Eat breakfast after waking up as soon as possible
- Get as much natural light outside as possible in the morning
- Training only in the morning.
- Dinner at the same time every day
- After 3 p.m., avoid coffee.
- After 4 p.m. no naps.
- Avoid food after 7 p.m. — have an early dinner
- Go to bed 2 to 3 hours before usual
- Limit the amount of evening light exposure
- Make sure your sleep and wake-up timings are the same every day

After the three-week study, results showed an increase in cognitive and physical performance during the morning hours, as well as a change in peak times from night to afternoon.

Researchers also noted that participants reported lower emotions of stress and depression. Participants succeeded in changing their body clocks for two hours during the study, the paper noted.

"Simple practices could help 'night' owls adjust their body clocks and improve general physical and mental health," said University of Surrey professor Debra Skene on Monday in a statement.

The multinational study also highlights the re-evaluation of burnout by the World Health Organization (WHO) as a sort of work-inducing stress. Burnout may be characterized as a sense of exhaustion of energy, increasing mental detachment from a person's job, or diminished professional efficiency according to WHO's new definition.

Compared to morning larks, senior study scientist Dr Elise Facer-Childs said that night owls tend to be more compromised in society since their schedules often are controlled by work or school commitments.

"We can make a long way in a society that faces constant pressure to achieve maximum productivity and performance by recognizing these differences and providing instruments for improving outcomes," said Facer-Childs, of Monash University's Turner Institute for Brain and Mental Health, in a statement.

A Final Word

You have been given the beautiful gift of time, and as the sun retreats and the moon rises to power, the hour is upon us to reap and sow its treasures, fly on, fellow night owl and thrive.

– Alexander Montrose

www.ingramcontent.com/pod-product-compliance
Lightning Source LLC
Chambersburg PA
CBHW070500220526
45466CB00004B/1905